W9-CYG-500

MANDALA MEDITATION

INTRODUCTION BY
LISA TENZIN-DOLMA

DUNCAN BAIRD PUBLISHERS
LONDON

Mandala Meditation
Introduction by Lisa Tenzin-Dolma

Distributed in the USA and Canada by Sterling Publishing Co., Inc.
387 Park Avenue South, New York, NY 10016-8810

This edition first published in the UK and USA in 2007 by
Duncan Baird Publishers Ltd
Sixth Floor, Castle House
75–76 Wells Street, London W1T 3QH

Copyright © Duncan Baird Publishers 2007
Text copyright © Duncan Baird Publishers 2007
Commissioned artwork copyright © Duncan Baird Publishers 2007

All rights reserved. No part of this book may be reproduced in any form or by
any electronic or mechanical means, including information storage and retrieval
systems, without permission in writing from the publisher, except by a reviewer
who may quote brief passages in a review.

Managing Editor: Kelly Thompson
Editor: Katie John
Managing Designer: Suzanne Tuhrim
Commissioned artwork: mandala color artworks by Sally Taylor/ArtistPartners Ltd;
line illustrations for mandala cards by Studio 73

Library of Congress Cataloging-in-Publication Data Available
ISBN-13: 978-1-84483-565-2   ISBN-10: 1-84483-565-0
10 9 8 7 6 5 4 3 2 1

Typeset in Lithos and Spectrum
Color reproduction by Colourscan, Singapore
Manufactured in China by Imago

Mandala Meditation is part of *The Mandala Coloring Kit* and must not be sold separately.

For information about custom editions, special sales, premium and corporate
purchases, please contact Sterling Special Sales Department at 800-805-5489 or
specialsales@sterlingpub.com.

Publishers' note: This book does not recommend meditation with mandalas for the
specific treatment of any disability, only for the enhancement of general well-being.
Meditation is beneficial for most people and generally harmless, but those unsure
of its suitability for them should consult a medical practitioner before attempting
any of the meditations in this book. Neither the publishers nor the author can
accept responsibility for any injuries or damage incurred as a result of following
the meditations in this book, or using any of the meditation techniques that are
mentioned herein.

CONTENTS

INTRODUCING MANDALAS

MANDALAS ARE SYMBOLIC PICTURES USED IN MEDITATION.
IMPORTANT IN MOST EASTERN TRADITIONS, THEY TAKE THE MEDITATOR
ON A WORDLESS JOURNEY INTO THE MIND'S DEEPEST MYSTERIES.

The designs of mandalas are formed from geometric shapes, sometimes with images of deities or natural forms included. The main shape is usually a circle, which symbolizes wholeness, and a cycle of energetic completion and renewal, as well as protection and healing. The circle may have squares and triangles set within or around it. When used in meditation, these shapes are designed to open up perception and to increase wisdom, compassion and a sense of communion between the self and the outer world.

The basis of all mandalas can be found in nature — in the whorl of a shell, the spiralling centre of a sunflower, the fullness of the sun, the symmetry of a snowflake and the ripples of a pond, to name but a few. Just like these natural forms, the shapes and symbols used in mandalas can evoke a deep appreciation of beauty, remind us of life's intricate harmony and bring about a sense of inner peace.

The circle of the mandala is a primal symbol for totality. It occurs in nature as the sun, giver of light, and the full moon, discloser of dark mysteries.

THE MANDALA TRADITION

THROUGHOUT HISTORY, MANDALAS HAVE BEEN USED IN DIFFERENT CULTURES AS A MEANS OF CONNECTING WITH THE WISE INNER SELF AND THE BENEVOLENT FORCES OF THE COSMOS.

People have created mandalas since the dawn of humanity, in the form of drawings and paintings on cave walls, to stimulate a feeling of connection with the environment and the animal kingdom.

In the East, especially in Buddhist and Hindu belief, mandalas form part of a long tradition of spiritual teaching. The word *mandala* comes from Sanskrit, the ancient holy language of India, and means "circle" or "centre". In Tibet, India and China, mandalas are widely used as a focus for meditation, to increase spiritual awareness. For the Kalachakra Initiation in Tibet, Buddhist monks create an intricate sand mandala that is dedicated to world peace. They use thin funnels to trickle coloured grains of sand in complex patterns. And, at the end of the ceremony, they sweep away the mandala, as a reminder of the impermanence of the material world.

The Aztec calendar is a religious mandala as well as an instrument for showing the passage of time. In Native American cultures, the mandala is echoed in the circular shape of medicine shields, which are designed to guide the spirit and empower the will. The circle also appears in dreamcatchers, which comprise a beaded and feathered web in a circular frame. Hung above a bed, they are designed to direct positive dreams into a sleeping person's mind, and to protect him or her by trapping negative dreams.

Although mandalas tend to be associated with the East, similar patterns have also existed throughout the history of the Western world. In Celtic tradition, knotwork and spiral patterns – intricate loops and whorls set within geometric shapes – trace paths that are designed to help to expand awareness. The Celtic Cross of the Christians, the "rosy cross" of the Rosicrucians, the circular labyrinth on the floor of Chartres Cathedral in France and the elliptical *vesica piscis* symbol – upon which many ancient sacred sites, such as Stonehenge, are based – also act as symbols to focus the mind. In addition, much sacred architecture around the world takes the form of mandalas: not just Buddhist stupas but also Christian cathedrals and Muslim mosques.

These and many other traditional mandalas are designed to symbolize the universe, reminding us of our place within the greater design of cosmic order.

MANDALAS AND MEDITATION

MANDALA MEDITATION INVOLVES FOCUSING YOUR ATTENTION GENTLY ON A MANDALA AND ALLOWING ITS EFFECTS TO BE FELT DEEPLY WITHIN YOURSELF.

Meditation helps you to calm the often overactive mind. There are many forms. You could use a mantra (a short word or other vocal sound), focus on a candle flame or just concentrate on the breath. This book teaches you to harness the power of mandalas – images composed of carefully arranged symbols and colours – to calm and deepen your awareness.

While the conscious mind tends to categorize what you see and experience via words, the unconscious mind understands symbols, responding to them with deep sensations and insights. Mandala meditation therefore opens a portal into the wise inner self, greatly enhancing self-understanding.

A mandala begins with a central point, which is the focus for your mind. The patterns that emerge from this point allow your mind to unfold gradually, like ripples spreading out from a stone that is cast into the still centre of a pond. The layers of symbols and colours are absorbed into your unconscious, and their beneficial effects occur naturally. You do not have to do anything – just "allow" them to happen.

Each mandala in this kit is designed for a specific purpose and helps to create a clear, peaceful space within you. You will be attracted to different mandalas at different times, as each picture bestows a unique insight. If you regularly meditate on mandalas, you will find that you can start to access the same sense of inner peace and harmony outside your meditation, too, thus improving your everyday life.

HOW TO MEDITATE ON A MANDALA

Allow at least five minutes and make sure you will not be disturbed. Sit on a chair, or cross-legged on a cushion.

1. Place the mandala of your choice about an arm's length in front of you, level with your line of vision.
2. Allow your attention to rest on the mandala, relaxing your gaze so that it is slightly out of focus.
3. Sit quietly, relax into the image and allow it to work on your mind. If thoughts distract you, or your gaze wanders, just bring your focus gently back to the mandala.
4. When you have reached the end of your meditation time, gently return your attention to the world around you.

COLOURS AND SYMBOLS

THE UNCONSCIOUS MIND NATURALLY RELATES TO SYMBOLS RATHER THAN WORDS. THE COLOURS, SHAPES AND IMAGES IN MANDALAS PROVIDE ACCESS TO A RICH SOURCE OF SPIRITUAL POWER.

The power of colour in influencing moods has been known for thousands of years. In Eastern traditions, colours are used in healing and meditation. Hindus and Buddhists identify seven subtle energy centres, called chakras, situated along the spine and in the head. Each chakra is associated with a different colour of the rainbow, starting with red as the base chakra, and progressing upward to violet for the crown chakra. The energy vibrations of different colours can be used or controlled to generate profound changes in your health and state of mind.

The German poet and mystic J.W. Goethe explored, in his book *Theory of Colour*, the ways in which colours affect the mind and body: for example, yellow made people feel warmer and blue made them feel colder. The influence of colour is even reflected in language: for example, people speak of "seeing red", being "green with envy" and "feeling blue".

This traditional Tibetan mandala, showing the goddess Vasudhara, is based on geometric shapes and strong colours, which unite the profusion of figures.

The following colours have been found to evoke specific feelings in people across many cultures. You may find that particular colours resonate with you.

- **Red** is the colour of blood and of life. It symbolizes vibrant energy, passion, determination, strength of will and motivation. It is also connected with anger.
- **Orange** is joyful and enlivening.
- **Yellow** stimulates the mind and aids concentration. It is also an uplifting colour, with a similar emotional effect to being outside in the sunshine.
- **Green** is restful and healing. It also signifies wealth, being the traditional colour of money.
- **Blue** has a cooling, calming effect.
- **Purple** represents spirituality, and features in many religious ceremonies. It is also used for ceremonial robes because of its associations with royalty.
- **Pink** is associated with gentleness, femininity and love. It can even calm angry or violent feelings.
- **Brown** suggests warmth, earthiness and stability.
- **White** symbolizes purity, as in angels' wings and fresh snow. It is also associated with peace.
- **Black** is the colour of death and the void. It also has connotations of mystery and austerity.

The shades within colours can also have different effects on the psyche. For example, a rich, deep shade of blue symbolizes insight, spirituality, devotion and calmness. A pale blue feels colder and signifies emotional detachment. And the blue of the sea makes people feel open and expansive.

Geometric shapes also have specific meanings for the unconscious mind. The following shapes, which commonly appear in mandalas, each tend to produce feelings that you can draw on in spiritual work.

- **The circle** represents wholeness and completion.
- **The spiral** is an open circle. It symbolizes natural, harmonious growth and expansion.
- **The square** signifies solidity and stability, firm foundations that can be built upon, and a sense of boundaries, encapsulation and containment.
- **The triangle** represents a state of striving toward perfection, and of intense focus.
- **A star** embodies hope, renewal and harmony.

Combinations of colours and shapes have different effects. For example, a red triangle represents life force and is likely to have you fizzing with energy and determination, a yellow triangle aids mental activity and concentration and a blue triangle can help you to feel calm and focused. When you meditate on any of the mandalas in this book, colour in one of the cards or even make your own mandala, notice the effects that different combinations have on you.

USING MANDALAS

BY WORKING WITH YOUR CHOSEN MANDALAS, YOU CAN GAIN
ACCESS TO ELEMENTS OF THE INNER SELF AT A FUNDAMENTAL LEVEL,
WHERE THEY EXIST IN UNITY AND HARMONY.

The mandala meditations in this book provide
a variety of symbols that you can tune into and
work with. Some, such as the Yin Yang and the Sri
Yantra, are derived from traditional Eastern imagery.
Others, such as the Endless Knot and the Snowflake,
are Western in origin or are modern creations.

Colouring in the mandalas on the cards is also a
meditative process. It helps you to focus your mind
on the essence of the mandala and allows the image
to become integrated easily and naturally into your
consciousness. The colours that you use do not have
to be the same as those of the corresponding mandala
in the book. You can select colours according to their
symbolism (see page 12). Alternatively, you can just
let yourself be guided by your intuition. Then, when
you look at your completed mandala, you may gain
insights into why you made the choices you did.

Colouring in a mandala centres and relaxes your
mind. It takes you into a still, pure space within
yourself, where thoughts drift away and there is a

sense of peace and fulfilment. If you wish, you can give your completed card to someone else, as a present. It will make a very special gift. As well as enjoying the beautiful image, the person receiving your card may choose to meditate on it, using it as a guide on a personal journey in which he or she can gain increased relaxation, clarity and insight.

SYMBOLIC IMAGES

Mandalas often contain pictures with specific spiritual meanings. Some of the images are familiar worldwide and appear in this book. Their messages can guide you as you meditate on, colour in or create a mandala.

• The yin-yang image embodies the dual nature of the cosmos: light and dark, form and formlessness, male and female. It can help you to reconcile different aspects of yourself and attain a sense of unity.

• Natural forms, such as flowers, trees, animals and the elements, enable you to connect with the natural forces that exist within yourself.

• The lotus, a spiritual symbol of enlightenment, has its roots in mud and silt, but its flower opens into the air. It reminds you that your roots, in the mud of the material world, anchor you and provide the nutrients that help you to blossom and develop the spiritual aspect of your character.

I A HEXAGRAM

THE HEXAGRAM IS A PAIR OF INTERLOCKING TRIANGLES,
REPRESENTING UNITY IN DUALITY. IN JUDAISM, THE SYMBOL IS
KNOWN AS THE STAR OF DAVID AND IS ALSO ASSOCIATED WITH
SOLOMON. HEXAGRAMS ALSO APPEAR IN HINDU MANDALAS.

1

Identify the upward-pointing triangle, which is masculine and symbolizes fire, and the downward-pointing one, which is feminine and denotes water.

2

Observe the upper part of the upward triangle, with the base of the downward triangle crossing through it: this is the symbol for air. Then observe the lower part of the downward triangle, again with a horizontal bar across it: this is the symbol for earth. The mandala, then, contains all four elements.

3

Take the mandala as a whole into your mind. As you do so, you are absorbing all the elements, all creation. The fifth element, spirit, denoted by the outer circle, is the medium through which your inner life unfolds.

"Those who worship Me with devotion, they are in Me and I am in them."

THE BHAGAVAD GITA (C.500BC)

2 YIN YANG

THE YIN-YANG SYMBOL AT THE CENTRE OF THIS MANDALA
IS AN ANCIENT EASTERN IMAGE. IT REPRESENTS THE BALANCE
BETWEEN OPPOSING FORCES THAT CONSTITUTES OUR WORLD.

1

Look at the flowers and other motifs set within the
main shapes. Appreciate the contrast of the squares
(the material world) with the circles (eternity).

2

Now look at the central yin-yang image. See how
each of the two elements contains the seed of its
opposite. Relate this idea to the opposites balanced
within you: masculine/feminine, action/stillness,
insight/compassion, outward/inward, and so on.

3

Look at the tiny yin-yang symbols and notice their
position, between the red square and the surrounding
circle, touching both. Think of them as atoms that
occur in everything, the universal stuff of existence.

4

See the mandala with all its embellishments as both
the cosmos and the individual cell – like life itself.

"Clay is fired to make a pot. The pot's use comes from its emptiness."

TAO TE CHING (4TH–3RD CENTURY BC)

3 THE ENDLESS KNOT

1

Become aware of the endless knot in the mandala
– the elaborately interlaced thread that has no
starting point. See this knot as a transcendental state
beyond the material world. Visually trace the thread
to satisfy yourself that it has no end.

2

Focus on the central cross within the circle – a
symbol of the physical (the cross) fused with the
spiritual (the circle).

3

Now let these two images – the encircled cross and the
endless knot – enter your mind as a single expression
of the eternal truth of existence: all existence is time-
bound, but ultimately it rests timelessly within the
divine or eternal spirit. Relax in this timelessness
throughout your meditation.

"*The end and the beginning of being are unknown.*
We see only the form in between. So what cause is there for grief?"

THE BHAGAVAD GITA (C. 500 BC)

4 A STAINED-GLASS WINDOW

THIS MANDALA EVOKES THE PEACE OF A CHURCH OR TEMPLE AND CAPTURES THE SUN'S RADIANCE: THE GIFT THAT BRINGS THE BEAUTY OF STAINED GLASS TO LIFE.

1

See the three- and four-leaved shapes as symbolic of nature – the universe of infinite forms. The subject of the window is the harmony of the natural world, shown by leaves, flowers and bunches of berries.

2

Start to see the pure design taking form as an actual window, which you are observing from inside a sacred building. Appreciate its artistry and workmanship.

3

Lastly, imagine that the window is lit from behind by bright sunlight. All the colours glow beautifully. The window has become a perfect symbol of nature animated by spirit and, at the same time, of human creativity animated by spiritual wisdom. As you draw the mandala deep into your mind, recognize that it reflects the essence of your true self.

"Truth and morning become light with time."

ETHIOPIAN PROVERB

5 ETERNAL FEMININE

THIS MANDALA ENCLOSES FEMININE SPIRITUALITY WITHIN
THE PROTECTIVE WALLS OF STRENGTH AND COMMON SENSE.
AT ITS CENTRE IS THE YONI, THE FEMALE CREATIVE SYMBOL,
HELD LOVINGLY WITHIN THE LOTUS OF ENLIGHTENMENT.

1

Look at the square around the lotus, with its double-buttressed walls. It is deeply set within the spiritual plane – the outer circle and the lotus buds, both of which suggest purity. The square is the foundation that grounds us and prevents us from losing touch with the eternal truth.

2

Let your mind enter the lotus flower and let the lotus flower enter you. While you are meditating upon this mandala, you are absorbing all the energies and essences of the eternal creative feminine principle, which brings you into the physical world and at the same time gives you the gift of intuitive wisdom.

"For a woman is the everlasting field in which the self is born."

THE MAHABHARATA (C. 400BC—AD 200)

6 ROSE OF PURE LOVE

THIS MANDALA IS THE ROSE CROSS, A SYMBOL THAT GAVE ITS NAME TO THE MYSTIC ORDER OF THE ROSICRUCIANS. THE CROSS IMPLIES THE FOUR CARDINAL DIRECTIONS, WHILE THE ROSE SUGGESTS PURE LOVE AS WELL AS SACRIFICE.

1

First, consider the cross, which anchors the spirit in the physical world. So powerful a symbol is the cross that we can readily imagine its central point behind the rose. It gives support to the rose, whose flowering transcends it.

2

Look at all the petals of the rose, beautifying the world. Think of them as the unfolding of love within your own heart.

3

Take the entire mandala into your inner self, where the rose will manifest selfless love, compassion and spiritual awareness.

"*The heart's message cannot be delivered in words.*"

MU-MON GENSEN (1322–1390)

7 DOVE OF PEACE

THE DOVE IS THE MOST SPIRITUAL OF BIRD SYMBOLS.
IN ADDITION TO ITS UNIVERSAL IMPORTANCE AS AN EXPRESSION
OF PEACE AND RECONCILIATION, IT CONJURES UP THE PURIFIED
SOUL – OR, IN CHRISTIAN TERMS, THE HOLY SPIRIT.

1

Within the outermost circle of the mandala, which indicates perfection, contemplate the continuous, flowing pattern as an image of earthly energies. The inner circles form a rainbow pattern, a beautiful manifestation of the life-giving spirit of the sun.

2

Now focus on the dove with its olive branch, a symbol of salvation. The dove has materialized out of pure spirit – like your own most profound qualities of love and peace. Hold the bird in your gaze as if you are seeing it through a telescope. The deep, dark background behind it is eternity.

3

Take this dove into your mind, and relax in the knowledge that it is completely at home there. You have recognized its sign, and you welcome the bird and its message of peace.

"Peace brings love as love brings peace. The perfect form is the circle."

MODERN MEDITATION FROM SYDNEY, AUSTRALIA

8 SRI YANTRA

THIS IS A SIMPLIFIED VERSION OF THE SACRED HINDU
SRI YANTRA. THE SRI YANTRA'S PATTERN OF INTERLINKING
TRIANGLES HAS A COMPELLING MYSTIC BEAUTY,
REPRESENTING THE TIMELESS CREATIVITY OF THE UNIVERSE.

1

Focus on the centre of the mandala and its opposing
sets of triangles – these interlocking shapes represent
the male and female principles, which, in their
fusion, give rise to all of creation.

2

Now turn your attention to the geometry
surrounding the image. Consider the equal-armed
cross, whose elements represent the created cosmos,
and the circle, denoting spiritual perfection.

3

Contemplate the centre of the Sri Yantra. This
point represents the source of all creation.
And your own mind, as it absorbs this yantra
into itself, is unfolding like everything else
in the cosmos, past, present and future, from
this transcendental, creative source.

"We meditate upon that divine sun, the true light of the shining ones.
May it illuminate our minds."

THE GAYATRI VERSE OF THE VEDAS (C. 5000BC)

9 HEART LOTUS

THE HEART IS THE MIDDLE POINT IN OUR SYSTEM OF CHAKRAS
(ENERGY CENTRES) WITHIN THE BODY. IT IS THE SOURCE FROM
WHICH LOVE AND COMPASSION EMANATE. THE LOTUS
SUGGESTS SPIRITUALITY, WHICH WE CAN FIND IN OUR HEARTS.

1

Look at the circle that frames the mandala – a symbol
of spiritual perfection.

2

Then contemplate the leaves and petals of the lotus,
which continue this symbolism. The lotus can
flower within ourselves and enable us to transcend
suffering. As we flower spiritually, our hearts spill
out love and compassion – tender as the lotus petals,
strong as the life-force itself.

3

Lastly, gaze at the central hexagram, with its
intersecting triangles, representing the dualities of
existence. To open the pure heart fully, we must
bring into balance the complementary aspects of our
life – male and female, light and shadow, mind and
body, practicality and spirituality.

"Heart is called the place where there is a repose in the pure light and pure consciousness."

ABHINAVAGUPTA (C.975—1025)

IO PERFECT SYMMETRY

THIS MANDALA, CENTRED ON THE PROMISE OF A FLOWER AND ITS SEEDS, CAN HELP THE MEDITATOR TO GO BACK SYMBOLICALLY TO THE MOMENT OF CREATION. IT REMINDS US THAT THERE IS NO FUNDAMENTAL DIFFERENCE BETWEEN SUBJECT AND OBJECT.

1

Appreciate the shapes of the mandala: start with the triangles, denoting the physical world, and turn next to the concentric circles, suggesting all-embracing spiritual perfection. Note also the "tear splashes" around the edges, suggestive of joy and sorrow.

2

Look at the triangles radiating from the middle in different directions. These represent the male and female principles that give rise, in their interplay, to creation. At the heart of the flower is a cluster of circles, like a seed head. These circles symbolize the divine source of all life, pulsing with energy, as if the sun had been squeezed to the size of a button.

3

Let all the energies of the mandala float deeper and deeper into your consciousness, until your mind achieves a perfect and peaceful resonance.

"*Everything in the universe is within you. Ask for everything from yourself.*"

JALAL AD-DIN RUMI (1207—1273)

II THE WORLD TREE

WITH ITS ROOTS AROUND THE EARTH AND ITS BRANCHES IN THE HEAVENS, THE WORLD TREE SYMBOLIZES OUR ABILITY TO TRANSCEND OUR HUMBLE ORIGINS IN THE DENSE REALM OF MATTER AND ASCEND TO HEAVENLY BLISS.

1

Contemplate the World Tree, so vast that its canopy stretches over day and night. The tree's fruits are the good things given to us by the divine – the harvest of virtues, including love, compassion, peace and self-awareness. In your knowledge of this tree, and of its fruits, you are immensely privileged. You are aware that, as long as you keep this knowledge in your heart, you will be fulfilling your true destiny.

2

Sense the vital essence of the World Tree, which is both material and spiritual, rising through the trunk and branches as you bring them deep into your mind, and flowing through the channels of your spirit.

3

Understand that if a branch breaks off, the tree still stands. In the same way, your spiritual essence is eternal, whatever accidents befall your body.

*"When the wind of pure thought rustles among its leaves,
the World Tree whispers the name of the divine."*

MODERN MEDITATION FROM GERMANY

12 A SNOWFLAKE

THE SNOWFLAKE IS FLEETINGLY BEAUTIFUL: WE SCARCELY
HAVE TIME TO ADMIRE IT BEFORE IT MELTS. SUCH IS THE WAY
OF THE WORLD: OUR LIVES AND LOVES CHANGE ENDLESSLY,
BUT AT OUR CENTRE IS THE UNCHANGING SPIRIT.

1

Look at the snowflake in this mandala, one of an
infinite number of snowflakes, yet complete and
perfect within itself. Observe its exact symmetry,
and be aware as you appreciate the design that no
other snowflake in the entire cosmos is identical to
this one. Let this thought sink into your mind. Spend
a few minutes relishing this everyday miracle.

2

Consider the snowflake's intrinsic strength, which
comes from its unique beauty. The snowflake is
ephemeral, yet flawless.

3

Imagine that the snowflake is on the point of melting.
You are observing it in the moment of its being,
from the viewpoint of your own fleeting lifetime.

"Weak overcomes strong, soft overcomes hard."

TAO TE CHING (4TH OR 3RD CENTURY BC)

ACKNOWLEDGMENTS

Many thanks and much love are offered to my family and friends, who are the shining lights of my life. Special thanks to Kelly Thompson, a real treasure of an editor; to Bob Saxton, the editorial director; and to the design team at DBP, who create such beautiful artwork. I hope that colouring the cards in this kit will bring you, the reader, great joy, and that the meditations and mandalas within the book will be a source of inspiration and a pathway to an increased sense of delight and self-discovery.

Lisa Tenzin-Dolma

PICTURE CREDITS

The publisher thanks the following people for permission to reproduce their material. Every care has been taken to trace copyright holders. However, if we have omitted anyone we apologize and will, if informed, make corrections to any future editions.
Page 4 Getty Images, London/Charles Krebs
Page 11 British Museum, London

Additional packs of the 12 mandala cards featured in this kit can be bought directly from the publishers. Please contact the Sales and Marketing Office, Duncan Baird Publishers, 29 Jewry Street, Winchester, Hampshire SO23 8RY
Tel: 01962 841 425   E-mail: enquiries@dbp.co.uk